MW00678751

MIMI AND MOTO
THE MOTORCYCLE MONKEYS
RIDE THE ALPHABET

BY NANCY GERLOFF AND MARK AUGUSTYN
ILLUSTRATED BY AVELIYA SAVINA AND MARAT KUROKHTIN
FOR FBT STUDIO

LITTLE RIDER ENTERPRISES

Aa

Our **alphabet adventure** begins with the great letter **A**.

As Mimi **and** Moto **always** like to say,

A is for **asphalt and ape-hangers** which **are awesome**.

Aunts are amazing, we **absolutely adore** them.

Bb

Our **big** letter **book** rolls on with **B**.
Boots and **brakes** and **bikers**, you see?
Brothers are the **best**, **believe** us we know.
Bring bananas and **burgers** to munch on the road.

Little riders go vroom, vroom
when they ride the alphabet so soon!

Cc

Enjoy the letter **C**, it is **classy** and proper,

like **cousins** on **cruisers** or shiny **chrome choppers**.

Can you say **curve**? **Could** you say **chain**?

Cafe racers wear **cool** goggles coming down **Center** and Main.

Dear little rider, our **day** continues with the **dandy** letter **D**.

Dirt bikes, **dual-sports** and **dads** rock, **do** you agree?

Dirty helmets and gloves most **definitely** protect.

Daddies teaching their **daughters** and sons to ride safe

deserve much respect.

Dd

Little riders go vroom, vroom
when they ride the alphabet so soon.

Ee

E is next in our alphabet soup with many **excellent** uses,

like **enduro** riders **exploring** the woods who make up no **excuses**.

Engines make your tires spin so you can go **extremely** far.

Two wheels make **everyone extra** happy so **enjoy**

and ride like a star!

F is most important for **family**, **friends** and **fans**.
It's also part of **fast** and **fun**, do you understand?
Mimi and Moto love **finishing first**, Kittie and Doggie love high **fives**.
The letter **F** is **fantastic** for **fixing** up **flat** track bikes.

Little riders go vroom, vroom
when they ride the alphabet so soon.

Ff

Gg

The starting **grid** needs the letter **G** and we are sure **glad** it is here,

just like **gorgeous grandmas** and **goofy grandpas** we love and hold so dear.

It's **good** for **gears** and **gas** which make you **go** and **go** and **go**!

Get your **gloves** and check your **gauges**, it's time to ride **great** roads.

Hh

The letter **H** is
for the **hill** climbs
that make your **heart**
beat **hard** and loud.
You need it for the
helmet you wear that
helps your **head** stay
safe and sound.
Horsepower and **headlights** make you **happy** on the
highways you may take, and **hold** those **handlebars** tight
in every **hairpin** turn you make.

Little riders go vroom, vroom when they
ride the alphabet so soon!

I is incredibly important when you eat yummy **ice** cream,

it is also for the **icky insects** on your windshield you must clean.

Insert the key **into** the **ignition** and travel many miles **in** a day,

imagine all the **interstates** you will see along your **interesting** way!

Ii

Jj

There is **joy** in **jumping** and **jumping** in **joy** and both sure need a **J**.
Amaze the **judges** with a **jillion** tricks so a trophy comes your way.
Want to **join** Kittie and Doggie for a **joyous jaunt** in **Japan**?
Would a **journey** in **June** or **July** sound like a **jolly** plan?

Little riders go vroom, vroom
when they ride the alphabet so soon!

Kk

K is for **kickstands** and **kickstarts** because both require a **kick**.

But sometimes **K's** are silent, just read and take your pick,

knee pucks, **knobby** tires and **knucklebusters** we **know**.

A **king** and queen seat **keeps Kittie** higher when two-up

under a rainbow.

We **like** the **letter L** for **left** and **lanes** and **lights**.
Mimi **loves** to wear racing **leathers**, they surely fit her tight.
Your **lean** angle will be **lower** with **lots** of practice on the track,
and your **lap** times will be faster **looking** forward, not back.

Little riders go vroom, vroom
when they ride the alphabet so soon!

Mm

Meet the **magical** letter **M**, it **makes** the **moon** and **moms** smile.

Motorcycles, **monkeys**, **Mimi** and **Moto**, it is **marvelous mile** after **mile**.

Motocross riders need **motors** to **move** around **muddy** tracks,

M is also **magnificent** when riding **mighty mountain** switchbacks.

Nn

Reykjavik

N comes **next** for the **nuts** which hold **nice** motorcycles together.
Nifty Kittie and Doggie use **N** when **navigating** their Iceland adventure.
New riders **need** help being **nimble** so the letter **N** is perfect **nearby**.
Never ever give up learning to read, **now** give it another try.

Little riders go vroom, vroom
when they ride the alphabet so soon!

Oo

Of course you must know the **outstanding** letter **O**,

just **open** your wise eyes and read.

Odometers, **off-road** motorcycles and **oil** need an **O**,

and **obviously** being **out** in the lead!

Pp

The letter **P** is **perfect** when **pistons** get **pushed** so **pass** the spark **plugs please**.
Purple pit bikes with **peppy pipes** in the **paddock**, Mimi and Moto **prefer plenty** of these.

Little riders go vroom, vroom
when they ride the alphabet so soon!

Qq

Say hello to the letter **Q**, a **quirky** letter it is true,
but **quite** needed if you like to ride **quickly**.
There is no **question** it is best, if you are on a **quest**
not to **quit** and learn to ride safely.

Rr

What would a **rusty rat** bike be without the letter **R**?

Where would all the **riders** go to **rally**?

Would you **remember** to slow down on **roads** in the **rain**?

Good thing **R** is always **revved** and **ready**.

Little **riders** go vroom, vroom

when they **ride** the alphabet so soon!

Ss

Mimi **says S stands** for **safety** which comes first in our **sport**.

Moto **says S** is for **supermoto**, a bike he **surely supports**.

Doggie **says S** is for the **sisters** that love **sportbikes** too.

Kittie says **S** is for **sidecars**. What **say** you?

Tt

Let's **talk** about **T**, **trust** us you'll see, it's another **tremendous** letter.
Touring bikes **traveling thousands** of miles, **truly there** is nothing better.
Trials bike riders **train** on **trails** day after day after day.
Top off your **tank**, fill up your **tires**, it is **time** to be on your way.

Little riders go vroom, vroom
when **they** ride **the** alphabet so soon!

Uu

Mimi and Moto stand **united** behind **U**, an **unbelievably useful** letter.

Uncles who **understand** motorcycles are **ultimately** much better.

When Moto makes a **u-turn**, he always watches the streets.

When Mimi rides **uphill** it makes her feel **upbeat**.

Very cool **vintage** motorcycles depend on the letter **V**,
just like a **visor** that shades your **view** so it is easier to see.
V-twin engines **vibrate** and rumble sort of like a **volcano**.
Studs are **vital** for **victory** when racing on ice and snow.

Little riders go **vroom**, **vroom**
when they ride the alphabet so soon!

Vv

Ww

Next in line comes the **wonderful** letter **W**,

without it **where would wild whoops** even be?

There could be no **winning, windshields** or **Wheelie Wednesdays**.

What if you **wanted** to just say **weeee**!?

The letter **X** is important if **mx** tracks sound good to you.
Want to play Tic Tac Toe in the dirt? **X** is good for that too.
Kittie and Doggie play the **xylophone** to relax after riding all day.
X marks the spot where our letter adventure continues on its way.

Little riders go vroom, vroom
when they ride the alphabet so soon!

Yes, with the great letter **Y you** can go the extra mile,

and ride **your yellow** motorcycle with attitude and style.

Y is perfect for sleepy **yawns** and eating **yummy** food.

Young little riders need rest and nutrition, is that understood?

Yy

The **zany** letter **Z**, oh how can it be, that our last letter has so much **zip**?

Adventure riders **zipping zippers** is a great way to end our alphabet trip!

So **zoom** off to your dreams little rider, where you can **zig** and **zag** around,

Catch some **zzz's**, it is time to sleep, Mimi and Moto will not make a sound.

Little riders go vroom, vroom

when they ride the alphabet so soon!

THE END.

THANK YOU!

Laura Shortridge - Joseph Romeo IV - Sasha A. Tcherevkoff - Olivia and Joey Behlmann - Zach and Fatema Grindell

Andrew Ciancia - Steve Hollister - Amy and Steven Becker - Christopher W. Blaich - Jenni Boynton

The Cunninghams - Alex and Jessie Hunter - River Bergstrom - Annette Harris - Uncle Zio Lusardi - Patrick Allos

Ania and Isla Osakowicz - Red and Chris Tanner - Slowinski Family - DeShawn Ingram - Kim Ong - Marlene

Stephen and Jeana Schupp - Kim Boyington - Karen Kelley and Shawn Filbey - James Kilkelly

Scott and Jennifer Pitts - Kogler Family - Jeff Roberts - John Chatters - Mike Norman - Bert and Carol Larsson

Craig M - Don and Jane Green - Matthew Brand - Tom Donohue - Skylar Turman - Tim, Katie, Luke and Spencer

Brett Kurtz - Sarah Schulz - WOW Motorcycles and Sky Hunter - The Mitchell Brothers - Anni Bossi

Leon and Marcy Hannum - Chris Price - Marilyn Stemp/Iron Trader News - Ryan, Brooke, Bentley, and Charlotte Shiel

Grandpa Dave and Grandma Chris Knoetgen - Evan Brady - Gustav Langer - Galen Haar - Daniel Weier

Widows Sons of Massachusetts - Tim and Carrie Wiseley - Christine McMahan and Larry Zagorski

Augusta, Oscar and Ian Wilson - The Camey Family - Stephen Phillipps - Scott and Davina Bledsoe - Jacob Badgley

Tim, Jane, and Vesper Clifton - Rhonda Travis Tucker - Randy and Natalie Tefft - Ryan Kennington

James "Bone" Turley - 360 Media, Inc. - Traci Zycha - Bart Rogowski and TST Industries - Lance Pare

Rosalie Calise and Sharon Myers - Tami Strahle - Micah Kauppila - Billy and Joyce Hitchcock - William Lighthart

Scott C. Stanley - Shannon Forst - Emilia and Antoni Augustyn - Egoavil Family - Michael Abbagnaro - Andrew Ramm

Kelly Van Allen - Belle Eloise Dickson - Maxden and Zaria TreeTop - Fafnir and Kiri - Jeff and Melissa Bixby

Mat Ward - Huelya Soeguet - Gabrielle and Malcolm Fontier - Miss Emma - David Moseley "Mo" - Harrison Holland

Brittany and Roger Marmol - Andrew Campbell - Christopher Peterson - Alex Arkhangelskiy - Carter Sexton

Shelby Drew - Creative Riding Podcast - Brian Goscinski Super Shox - MyFirstRide.org and Motorcycles.org

Sally "Mimi" Yost - Tony Nassisi - Maddy Lee Johnson - Barrett and Piper Smith - Brice Walk

Alyse's "Mimi" Janell Stangl - Owen L. Riess - Ayla Jane Carroll - Debra Slicer - Jeffrey Chandler - Gene

Arianna and Laurence Shapiro - River Novic - Paul Lynch and Family - Andrew C.S., Angela C.S., and Dan S.

Linda and Freddy Bailey - Jared, Nichole and Hayden Mees - Motorsavage - Nikki Cherokee

Text and Illustration Copyright© 2019 Nancy Gerloff and Mark Augustyn

Illustrations and Design by Aveliya Savina and Marat Kurokhtin for fbtstudio.com

Creative Direction by Esteban Alvarado

All rights reserved. No part of this book may be reproduced in any manner whatsoever without
written permission except in the case of brief quotations embodied in critical articles and reviews.

Printed in The United States of America.

10 9 8 7 6 5 4 3

ISBN 978-0-578467-48-1

Published by Little Rider Enterprises

www.mimiandmoto.com